COURTSIDE
COMPANION

John Zwieg's

COURTSIDE COMPANION

a tennis workbook for the serious player
edited by Richard S. Isaacs

 CHRONICLE BOOKS/SAN FRANCISCO

Printed in the United States of America
ISBN 0-87701-042-0
Library of Congress Catalog Card No. 73-77334

contents

preface

Historically the game of tennis has known many great players, teachers of recognized capability and a number of writers who have represented the skills of both the player and the teacher.

However, as the game of tennis spurts forward into the 1970's with a momentum almost unparalleled by any other sport, the demand for competent instructors has outrun, in many areas, the availability of such professionals. And as a result there are many serious players who are either working on their own or with only an opportunity for occasional help from a qualified instructor.

Because of these factors, and because even the most proficient player needs to constantly check his grip, his stance and his technique, there is a very real need for an illustrated book to fill this void. This book, illustrating the teaching technique of John Zwieg, who in addition to being an excellent teacher is also a fine player, should be a most welcome addition to the growing resource of tennis knowledge.

Barry MacKay

Former National Amateur Champion
Five times U.S. Davis Cup Team Member

introduction

The *Courtside Companion* is a tennis workbook for the serious player. It is not the autobiography of a tennis celebrity nor is it the detailed account of a successful teacher reviewing the past triumphs of his students.

It is not designed to compete with or supplant any existing tennis work. Yet it does have a place on the library shelf or at court-side of any serious player.

You are a tennis champion when you have trained yourself to play up to the limit of your native ability.

Depending upon your age, sex, inherent physical characteristics, training and desire, you may find yourself suffering from centercourt jitters at Forest Hills or side-court fright in your challenge on the C-class ladder at your home court. It doesn't matter. What does matter is that you live up to the challenge and excitement of knowing that you are doing the very best you can.

This is both the sport and the spirit underlying my philosophy of tennis instruction. And it's the reason you'll be a better tennis player if you work with the *Courtside Companion* on a regular basis. Prop it up on a chair at courtside or in front of a mirror while you attempt to duplicate the illustrations. If your club is so equipped, have films made of you and compare them with stop action photos in the book.

There are no shortcuts to personal achievement in tennis. It is not a team sport. So when you are out on the court, your success or failure is totally dependent upon you. There's no place to hide.

But when you have developed your skills to the limit of your ability, you won't have to hide because at that moment in time and in your tennis playing life you are, by definition, a champion.

basic conditioning

This book makes no attempt to outline a serious program for physical conditioning. It is not a course in physical education. If you are interested in such programs, there are many outstanding books on the subject. Consult them.

Listed here are but a few helpful hints on the types of exercise that will be useful to you in preparing for the game of tennis. Add to it as your own physical make-up dictates.

Run in place indoors or jog in a convenient location outdoors. Begin with a half-mile jaunt and work up to longer distances over a period of time. Running will increase respiration and endurance. As your condition improves, add short sprints to your roadwork.

Push-ups will strengthen the pectoral (chest) muscles which in turn will help in your serve, overhead and ground strokes.

Skipping rope will aid in balance and foot reflex.

Kangaroo hops will condition legs and prevent "leg drag."

Hand squeezing mechanisms, such as a squash ball, will do wonders for the wrist and forearm.

Sit-ups are good for strengthening shoulder, pelvic and abdominal muscles.

Touch your toes. An old standard, but a good one for both circulation and the waistline.

Remember, start slowly and increase each exercise as your physical condition warrants. Never strain.

selecting equipment

Selecting and buying equipment is a very personal act. The way it looks to you, its feel, the balance, even color—all combine to make a purchase *the right purchase.*

Listen to a reliable tennis instructor or club professional; his guidance will be good. But don't buy a certain type of racket because a great professional, or your friend, uses it. The racket may be absolutely correct for them, but not for you.

Wood versus metal. Normally wood will give a player more control over the ball, but less power. Conversely, a metal racket will give more power but less control. These are not absolutes, however. Actual play will provide the proof in your particular case.

And whether wood or metal is of little consequence without the proper strings. So always buy an *unstrung* racket and have it strung by a professional.

Gut strings will provide more resiliency and control; *nylon* of good quality is ideal for damp weather.

Wood rackets should be strung with a tension of 60 to 65 pounds; metal rackets should be given a tension of 55 to 60 pounds.

Balance may be key to performance. Choose a racket that isn't top heavy. If a racket is too heavy, it is difficult to control. It is best to consult a club tennis pro or other qualified instructor if you feel unsure.

Grips range from 4 inches to 5 inches in circumference. Again, no exact formula is possible because so much depends upon an individual's hand size.

I feel that except for the exceptionally strong man, a player should choose a lightweight racket. Weights run about as follows:

Lightweight	11 to 13 oz.
Medium	13½ to 13¾ oz.
Heavy	14 to 15 oz.

Balls. If you live or are to play in high altitudes, purchase "box" or non-pressurized balls. For all other locations, purchase pressurized balls in a can.

Proper dress. The traditional tennis attire for both sexes is white: shoes, sox, shorts, shirt and jacket. The ladies may opt for a tennis dress in place of shorts and shirt, if they wish. However, with the ever-increasing popularity of exhibition tennis, color is gradually coming to the courts. But to be on the safe side remember that white is always acceptable and, more often than not, preferred.

When in doubt, or when visiting another club, inquire about their requirements. In this way you will avoid embarrassment for both you and your host.

learning and perfecting
the basic strokes

the forehand

learning and perfecting the basic strokes

the forehand

The forehand is the first, basic stroke to be learned. Without it, other strokes, no matter how well perfected, become less of a threat and, as such, less effective.

There have been many great players known for their execution of a stroke other than the forehand but, in every instance, these players had perfected a reliable forehand. No one ever said, 'Ken Rosewall has a great backhand but a poor forehand.' Or that Pancho Gonzales was, in his prime, the master of the serve, but his forehand let him down. The same for Lew Hoad and the volley. Each may have had a favorite crowd pleaser, but the greatness of that special shot was made more effective by a strong, reliable forehand.

Slice it. Hit it with topspin. Lob. Drop shot. Hit it down the line or crosscourt. Soft or hard. All are shots that can be done off the forehand—with practice. So practice until the stroke becomes a part of you; until it is correctly executed without conscious effort, by reflex.

The forehand is the foundation for an aggressive, winning game. Make it your ally.

The highspeed photographic sequence shown above demonstrates a properly executed forehand. Study it carefully. Now turn the page and follow the step-by-step breakdown of the stroke from grip to followthrough. Then return once again to this illustration to seat the proper technique firmly in your mind. Best of all, imitate the action, stopping your motion at each stage to compare your position with that in the corresponding photograph.

the forehand (step by step)

1 The Grip

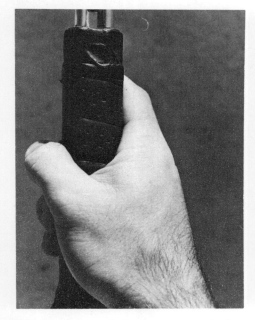

The Eastern grip is recommended for best results. Here is how you achieve it: (1) shake hands with the racket as you would shake hands with a friend; (2) place the hand so that the space between the thumb and index finger forms a "V" on the top of the racket; (3) be certain the hand is in the middle of the leather; and, (4) position the index finger knuckle on the outside of the racket.

2 Ready position

Face the net, feet straight ahead and shoulder-width apart. Flex your knees and bend forward slightly at the waist. Using finger tips, place your non-hitting hand on the throat of the racket with the racket head level with your chin. Flex elbows slightly to keep the racket comfortably in front. Keep weight forward on the balls of your feet.

3 Straight back turn

Turn on the balls of your feet, elevating the heel of the foot opposite the racket hand as you pivot. While rotating your shoulders, torso and hips, bring the racket straight back to knee-low. Halfway between the ready position and a complete turn, drop your non-hitting hand to assure a sideways position. Keep the wrist firm and set back, the shoulder stiff and the elbow bent.

4 Circular motion turn

A somewhat more advanced technique incorporates the circular motion turn. Properly executed, it provides more rhythm and speed to the ball. Instead of bringing the racket back knee-low, turn on the balls of the feet, rotate the shoulders, torso and hips, and blade the racket back by your ear. Then drop it to knee-low. Keep the wrist firm and set back, the shoulder stiff, the elbow bent.

5 Move to ball
Straight back motion

Transfer your weight onto the front foot at about a 45° angle as you turn toward the net. This will thrust your weight into the ball. Be sure to step with the toe leading, rather than the side of the foot, to permit the body to rotate smoothly into the ball as it bounces toward you. The hit comes as the racket is brought around from in back and slightly below the knee and moves upward in a gradual plane.

6 Move to ball
Circular motion

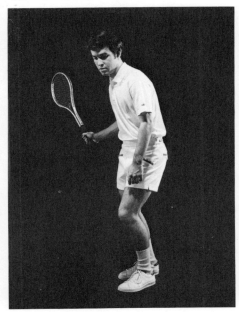

The fundamentals are the same as for the straight back motion except that the racket head comes around, down and into the ball in a circular motion, building more speed and momentum as it goes.

7 Step and hit

Contact is made with the racket even with the front toe. The wrist is set back, shoulders stiff and eyes on the ball. Remember, the racket comes around when your body comes around.

8 Followthrough

Reach toward the net, lift at the knees and hit through the ball. Your weight should be centered over the front foot. The racket finishes head-high in the direction of the shot. Ideally, for more control, the racket and the ball should be in contact no less than 24 inches in the forward movement toward the net. Lifting the knees for the follow-through will give the ball topspin.

the forehand (footwork)

1 the Hit close to the body

Take racket back. As the ball approaches close to your body, turn, bringing the right foot back parallel to the baseline.

2 Step and hit

Having kept the weight off the stepping foot as much as possible, step in and hit.

3 Hit slightly away from the body

Racket back. Step out with the right foot parallel to the baseline. This will move you into the ball.

4 Hit far from the body

Again lead with the right foot. Take quick crablike steps toward the ball. Set quickly, step and hit. It is best to take small steps.

5 Hitting the high, deep ball

Sidestep with the right foot back toward the fence. Racket back. Now let the ball drop to waist-high as you shift the weight forward on the left foot. On extremely high balls, try to drive your return deep.

6 Step and hit

Shift the weight forward on the left foot and hit.

7 Hitting the short ball

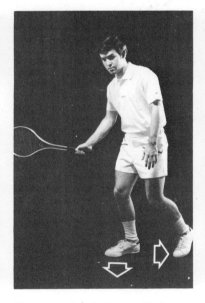

Do not attack the ball directly. Move into the ball at an angle. Sidestep with the left foot and move toward the ball with the right foot.

8 Step and hit

The final step with the left foot should be the *hit* step. Be certain to shorten your back swing to about half normal to reduce racket momentum.

9 Followthrough

Always make a complete followthrough.

the backhand

The backhand is a more natural stroke than the forehand. This is true despite the fact that it is often the inexperienced player's greatest weakness. The reason may be this: On the forehand stroke the player must hit *around* his body, while with the backhand stroke, there is no body to interfere with the natural, smooth flow of the stroke.

Properly developed and practiced, this stroke not only ceases to be a weakness and a point of competitive vulnerability, it be-

comes a potent weapon on attack. Many times it is the stroke used to set up a winning shot with the forehand.

The highspeed, photographic sequence shown above, illustrates how the complete stroke should look. Use it as your checkpoint. Return to it often as you practice the step-by-step execution of the backhand illustrated on the next pages.

the backhand (step by step)

1 The Grip

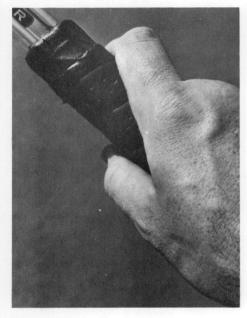

For the quickest and surest positioning, start with the forehand grip, then make a ¼ turn of the top shaft of the racket. As you look down, it should look directly back at you.

2 Ready position

Face the net, feet straight ahead and shoulder-width apart. Flex the knees and bend slightly forward at the waist. Using finger tips, place your non-hitting hand lightly on the throat of the racket with the racket head level with your chin. Now flex elbows slightly to keep the racket comfortably in front. Keep forward on the balls of your feet.

3 Straight back turn

The straight back motion is a preliminary move. Turn on the balls of your feet. Rotate shoulders, torso and hips, bringing racket back to knee-low. The right shoulder should point to the net. Keep the wrist firm and set back. Arms should be stiff with the right thumb near the left upper leg.

4 Circular motion turn

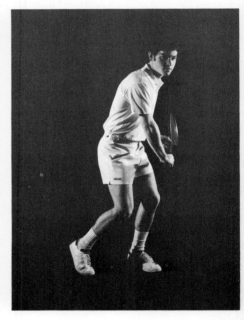

To achieve more rhythm and speed to the ball, turn on the balls of the feet, rotate the shoulders, torso and hips, and bring the racket head back to about waist-high by bending both elbows slightly.

5 Move to ball
Straight back motion

Step toward the net with the front foot at about a 45° angle. Bring the racket around using shoulders, torso and hips. Arms remain straight, wrists firm. Shift weight to the front foot. Be careful to lead with the toe, not the side of the foot, as you step to allow for a smooth rotation into the ball.

6 Move to ball
Circular motion

From the initial backswing, bring the racket to knee-low by extending the arms straight. Rotate the shoulders, torso and hips around to the ball.

7 Step and hit

Now with your front foot at a 45° angle and your body properly rotated, your racket should be even with the front foot where contact is made. Unlike the forehand, the elbow should remain straight. The racket is even with the hand. Eyes on the ball.

8 Followthrough

From the followthrough you achieve both direction and control. From the hit, reach toward the net so that the ball is in contact approximately 24 inches. Lift the knees to give topspin to the ball. The weight should be centered over the front foot when the stroke is complete.

the backhand (footwork)

1 Hit close to the body

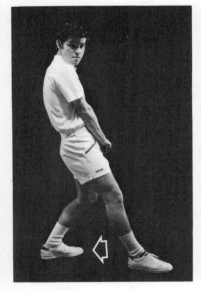

Take racket back. As the ball approaches, close to your body, turn, bringing the left foot back parallel to the baseline.

2 Step and hit

Having kept the weight off the stepping foot as much as possible, step in and hit.

3 Hit slightly away from the body

Racket back. Step out with the left foot parallel to the baseline. This will move you into the ball.

4 Hit far from the body

Again lead with the left foot. Take quick crablike steps toward the ball. Set quickly, step and hit. It is best to take small steps.

5 Hitting the high, deep ball

Sidestep with the left foot back toward the fence. Racket back. Now let the ball drop to waist-high as you shift the weight forward on the right foot. On extremely high balls, try to drive your return deep.

6 Step and hit

Shift weight forward onto the right foot and hit.

7 Hitting the short ball

Do not attack the ball directly. Move into the ball at an angle. Sidestep with the right foot and move toward the ball with the left foot.

8 Step and hit

The final step with the right foot should be the *hit* step. Be certain to shorten your back swing to about half normal to reduce the racket momentum.

9 Followthrough

Always make a complete followthrough.

the serve

The serve initiates play. It can be delivered flat. Sliced. With spin. Hard or soft.

At times it has been called the "hammer" which, of course, connotes power rather than finesse. The importance of the serve is variously regarded by different professionals. No matter. What is important is a recognition of the fact that there is no substitute for a reliable first serve and a second serve over which you have unfailing control. Only then can you keep your opponent on the defensive, permitting you to play *your* game.

With the serve you control court position of your opponent. This is done by a combination of *placement* and *speed* rather than simply excessive power.

A properly executed serve, as shown above, will permit you to take advantage of your forehand and backhand and, for that matter, all the strokes in your repertoire. Study it carefully before turning to the step-by-step discussion.

the serve (preliminary and half serve)

1 The Grip

Place the index finger between the forehand and the backhand grips. Hold the racket in the center of the leather. This grip will give a natural spin to the serve.

2 The Toss

Hold the ball between the thumb, forefinger and middle finger at the tips. The ball should not touch the palm of the hand. The palm should point toward the side fence, not upward.

3 Full vertical toss

Toss the ball vertically and release at full extension of the arm. The momentum of the arm from thigh to full extension is enough to propel the ball into position. Properly executed, body weight will shift forward.

4 Ready position

Assume a stance sideways to the net, with the back foot parallel to the baseline. Place the front foot close to the baseline, with the left toes always pointing to the right net post. The racket position is behind the player, with the elbow raised to about shoulder height and the hand behind the ear.

5 Downward arm action

The back foot instep is opposite the heel of the front foot and about shoulder-width apart. The throwing arm moves down to the left thigh. The weight is distributed evenly on both feet.

6 Upward arm action

As the arm extends to a vertical position over the front toe, shift your weight forward to the front foot, allowing the heel of the back foot to raise.

7 Reaching for the ball

Begin the extension of the forearm and racket to the ball. Start rotation of shoulders, torso and hips over the front foot.

8 Contact

With arm at full extension at about one o'clock, snap wrist down and through the ball. Your body should be almost square to the net.

9 Downward action

Continue to drive shoulders, hips and torso around, bringing the racket head downward. This action will bring your back foot around naturally.

10 Followthrough

The right foot should move across the baseline to take your weight as the racket head completes its arc, ending up on the left side of the body. The serve completed, move quickly to ready position.

the full serve (step by step)

1 Ready position

Assume a sideways position to the net with left toes pointing to the right net post. The racket and arms are held in front of the body in the direction of the serve, about waist-high and lined up over the front foot.

2 Down swing

Keeping in mind the old phrase "down together, up together," start both arms downward in a slow, comfortable motion. Weight should be evenly distributed on both feet. Wrist is firm. The tossing arm is lined up over the front toes, the racket arm just passes the right leg.

3 Begin upswing

Begin "up together" motion, raising the left arm out over the front toe and the racket arm upward from the right side. Weight is beginning to shift forward.

4 Mid-point upswing

The tossing arm is approaching vertical position and is still lined up over the front toe. The racket is upward in a vertical position and the wrist is firm.

5 Upswing completed

You have now reached the "up together" point of the serve. The tossing arm is vertical over the front toe and the racket arm is back. The wrist drops slightly. In this position as the ball is released the weight is on the front foot.

6 Move to the ball

Reach up toward the ball and begin to drive shoulders, torso and hips from the right side.

7 Contact

With the arm fully extended and palm down, make contact with the ball at its zenith and out in front.

8 Begin followthrough

Snap the wrist through the ball. Continue to drive the right shoulder, torso and hip around. The back foot begins to come forward. Continue the long reach toward the net.

9 Continue followthrough

Continue body rotation until square with the net.

10 Complete followthrough

Finish the stroke with the racket on the left side. Body has come around. Back foot has come into the court. The followthrough complete, move quickly to the ready position behind the baseline.

forehand volley

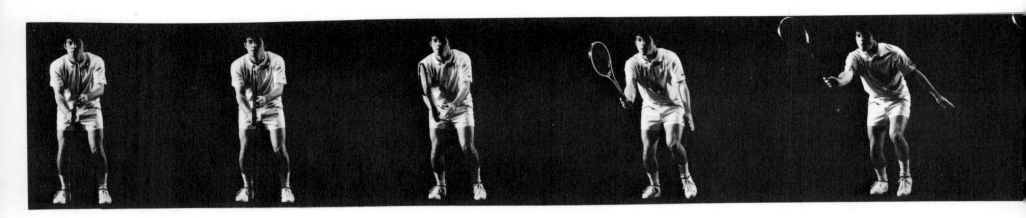

backhand volley

A volley is simply *a ball hit on the fly.* It is a stroke most often executed in the vicinity of the net, although it may be hit from any position on the court.

For the purposes of discussion in this section, only the net volley will be covered. Later sections will deal with such variations as the half volley, lob volley and drop volley.

The advantages of the net volley are several: It takes the pace off the ball. It shortens the court. It widens the angle of the court. And it gives your opponent less time to get set which should often result in your delivering a winner.

Carefully study the highspeed photographic examples shown here before moving to the step-by-step discussion.

31

forehand volley (step by step)

1 Ready position

Assume the regular ready position but crouch slightly lower. Use your regular forehand grip in the beginning stages, keeping in mind that you may wish to use just one basic grip (the serve grip) for all volleys.

2 Move to the ball

Start the racket above the line of the ball. There is little backswing on the volley, but a slight pull to the side of the body. The racket head always stays above the wrist. Line the ball up with the racket face. When in the correct position, the racket head will be positioned at about 2 o'clock.

3 Volley contact

Keeping the racket at about 2 o'clock, make contact well out in front. Endeavor to have the ball "sit" in the strings. Use slight shoulder and forearm action to punch the ball down and out. The wrist should be kept firm. On exceptionally hard hit balls merely block the ball with your racket.

4 Followthrough

Complete the stroke with the racket head above the net tape and in front. There is no long step or followthrough on the volley as there is with the ground strokes.

backhand volley (step by step)

1 Ready position

Assume the regular ready position but slightly crouched. Use your regular forehand grip in the beginning, then change to the backhand grip. Keep your eyes on the ball.

2 Move to the ball

Start the racket above the line of the ball. As the ball approaches, line it up as though you are going to catch it with your left hand. As the racket is taken back slightly, the left hand is placed on the throat of the racket.

3 Volley contact

Make contact well out in front of the body. The left hand should be released. Try to have the ball "sit" in the strings. Use slight shoulder and forearm action to punch the ball down and out. Keep wrist firm. The racket head is above the waist at about a 10 o'clock position.

4 Followthrough

After contact, the racket head should continue through the ball and about 18 inches farther than with the forehand followthrough, but still above the net.

the overhead

The overhead is an often neglected stroke, primarily because many players consider it a power play rather than a placement weapon.

It is a crowd pleaser when well-executed, but more often than not fails because it is improperly used. In this discussion, it is treated as just one more tool needed by the complete player.

Viewed in its proper context, it is the stroke that is needed to complement the volley in your net game.

Because of the degree of difficulty in executing the overhead, it will require proportionately longer hours of practice. Give it this attention.

the overhead (step by step)

1 Ready position

Assume the volley ready position. Move to the service grip. Remember, the overhead results from your net play, you do not control it.

2 Overhead position

Once the lob has been hit, you must position yourself sideways to the net. Your racket must be held in an upward position. Your feet are in the serve position, left foot in front of your right, spread about shoulder-width. You may use your non-hitting arm to point to the ball which will help to keep the ball out front.

3 Drop racket down

This move is like cocking a gun. The non-hitting arm is still pointing toward the ball. The body weight has not yet shifted forward.

4 Reach to the ball

The move to the ball now begins. The racket arm has come out of its cocked position. Weight is shifting forward onto the left foot. The ball should be well out in front.

5 Full extension

This is the point of maximum reach to the ball. Eyes should be fixed directly on the ball. Weight is shifted forward. Shoulders, torso and hips should begin to rotate from the right side.

6 Contact point

Contact is made in front of the body. The wrist snaps to the ball while the right shoulder, hips and torso continue to come around. Weight is on the front foot.

7 Begin followthrough

Player should continue a long reach to the back fence while his shoulders, torso and hips come around hard. The wrist has brought the racket through the ball.

8 Followthrough

At the finish, shoulders, torso and hips have come completely around and the back foot has come through to take the weight. The racket arm finishes on the left side. Move back to your volley ready position.

the overhead (backhand)

The backhand overhead is a most difficult shot to put away. Most players use it sparingly because they feel unsure in hitting the stroke. It finds its greatest acceptance as a placement vehicle. It takes both practice and patience to master.

1 Move to the ball

Assume the volley ready position. (At the outset, a player will find it easier to use the backhand grip.) Move the racket head to the overhead position. Keep both arms straight. Place the left hand on the racket shaft and turn body sideways to the net. Be certain the racket head is positioned square to the ball.

2 The Hit

Remove the left hand and bring the racket head to the ball. Snap the wrist downward while beginning rotation of shoulders, torso and hips. Keep weight forward.

3 Followthrough

Complete rotation of shoulders, torso and hips. Racket head will finish on the right side. Immediately return to ready position.

the lob

The lob is both an offensive and a defensive stroke, depending upon the situation.

Offensively, it could be considered a third passing shot. It is an all-court stroke.

Defensively, it is used to get out of trouble. By hitting the ball high, you give yourself time to re-establish good court position.

Key to the lob's success is to loft it high over your opponent so that he cannot return it as an overhead, but must assume a defensive attitude.

forehand topspin lob

1 The Backswing

Move into your normal forehand stroke. Racket back, body sideways to the net.

2 Move to the ball

Start to move shoulders, torso and hips around. Advance racket head to the ball, keeping it slightly below the wrist.

3 Contact

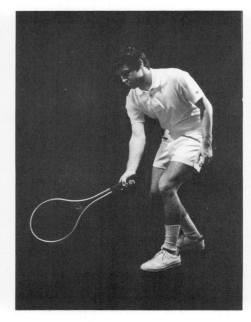

Position the racket head behind the ball and hit out in front of the forward toe.

4 Followthrough

Raise the knees and swing upward to give the ball a forward spin and rotate the wrist through the ball. Finish high over the head in a smooth motion.

forehand underspin lob

1 The Backswing

Move into your normal forehand stroke. Racket back knee-low, body sideways to the net.

2 Move to the ball

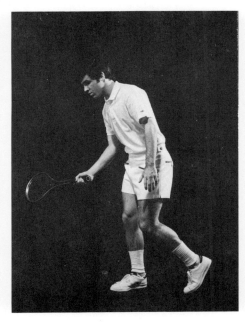

Position racket head very low. Open the face to allow the lower portion of the frame to lead into the ball. Backward spin will result.

3 Contact

Contact should be made out in front of the forward foot, with the racket open and just below the wrist.

4 Followthrough

Carry the ball on the racket upward in a forward plane. Raise the knees upward and finish with the racket head-high.

backhand topspin lob

1 The Backswing

Move into the normal backswing from the ready position, body sideways to the net, arms straight.

2 Move to the ball

Bring the racket head around just below the wrist. Drop the leading shoulder. Weight begins to move forward.

3 Contact

The racket head should be positioned well out in front of the leading foot. Arms straight. Racket head below the wrist. Weight forward.

4 Followthrough

Deliver the racket head from behind the ball upward in a forward plane, to give the ball topspin. Come up with knees and continue the followthrough high over the head in a smooth motion.

backhand underspin lob

1 The Backswing

Move into the normal backswing from the ready position, body sideways to the net, arms straight.

2 Move to the ball

Bring the racket head around just below the wrist. Drop the front shoulder. Weight begins to come forward. Now bring the racket into contact with the ball in an open face position so that the lower part of the frame leads into the ball.

3 Contact

Move the racket head under the ball with the open face of the racket head to apply backspin.

4 Followthrough

Carry the ball on the racket and come upward with the knees. Bring the racket in a forward plane, finishing head-high.

return of serve

Accomplished players, both professional and amateur, will agree that the return of serve is as important as the serve itself. Like a boxer using the jab to set up the big punch or a combination, the tennis player must jab with the return of serve until he is in a position to move to the offense. If you have a weak serve it is all the more important that you develop a reliable return of serve. With this weapon, you take the uneven advantage of the big serve away from your opponent.

forehand return of serve (deuce court)

1 Ready position

Assume the standard ready position for the forehand. Position yourself inside the baseline, equidistant from the singles sideline and the center service line. Study your opponent's game and plan accordingly: for a high-spin bounce hold the racket head high; for low hard serves, hold it more at the knees or waist.

2 The Backswing

Observe the ball in flight and before it bounces, take the racket back to your side. The body should be slightly turned. If you find you are turning late, position yourself behind the baseline to give yourself more time.

3 Move to the ball

Bring the racket head forward with the motion of the shoulder, torso and hips, acting simultaneously with the front foot's forward motion. Hold wrist firm. Left hand in slightly, and racket head even with the hand.

4 The Hit

With the wrist held firm make contact out in front of the stepping foot. Keep eyes directly on the ball. Carry the racket head and ball in a straight line with a push action to assure more control to the return. Don't pull up. The weight should be completely forward.

5 Followthrough

Hold the followthrough just out in front, reaching toward the net. Then start your move back to the center of the court, using the proper footwork.

forehand return of serve (ad court)

1 Ready position

Assume the standard ready position for the forehand. Position yourself inside the baseline, equidistant from the singles sideline and the center service line. Study your opponent's game and plan accordingly: for a high-spin bounce hold the racket head high; for low hard serves, hold it more at the knees or waist.

2 The Backswing

Observe the ball in flight and before it bounces, take the racket back to your side. The body should be slightly turned.

3 Move to the ball

Bring the racket head forward with the motion of the shoulders, torso and hips and in rhythm with the front foot's forward motion. Hold the wrist firm, pull the left hand in slightly and keep the racket head even with the hand.

4 The Hit

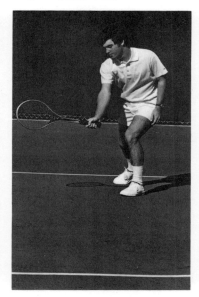

With the wrist held firm, make contact well in front of the stepping foot. Keep eyes directly on the ball. Carry the racket head and the ball in a straight line with a push action to assure more control. Don't pull up with the body. Weight should be completely forward.

5 Followthrough

Hold the followthrough out in front, reaching for the net. Then move quickly back to center court.

backhand return of serve (deuce court)

1 Ready position

Assume the ready position. Position yourself inside the baseline, equidistant from the singles sideline and the center service line. Study your opponent's game and plan accordingly: for a high-spin bounce hold the racket head high; for low hard serves, hold it more at the knees or waist.

2 The Backswing

Observe the ball in flight and before it bounces, take the racket back to your side. The body should be slightly turned. If you find you are turning late, position yourself behind the baseline to give yourself more time.

3 Move to the ball

Bring the racket head forward with the motion of the shoulders, torso and hips in rhythm with the front foot's forward motion. Hold the wrist firm, pull the right hand in slightly and keep the racket head even with the hand.

4 The Hit

With the wrist held firm, make contact out in front of the stepping foot. Keep eyes directly on the ball. Carry the racket head and ball in a straight line with a pull action to assure more control to the return. Don't pull up. The weight should be completely forward.

5 Followthrough

Hold the followthrough just out in front, reaching toward the net. Then start your move back to the center of the court, using the proper footwork.

backhand return of serve (ad court)

1 Ready position

Assume backhand ready position. Position yourself inside the baseline, equidistant from the singles sideline and the center service line. Study your opponent's game: if he has a high-spin bounce, hold the racket head high; if he delivers a low, hard serve, hold the racket head more at the knees or waist.

2 The Backswing

Observe the ball in flight and before it bounces, take the racket back to your side. The body should be slightly turned. If you find you are turning late, position yourself behind the baseline to give yourself more time.

3 Move to the ball

Bring the racket head forward with the motion of the shoulders, torso and hips in rhythm with the front foot's forward motion. Hold the wrist firm, pull the right hand in slightly and keep the racket head even with the hand.

4 The Hit

With the wrist held firm, make contact out in front of the stepping foot. Keep eyes directly on the ball. Carry the racket head and ball in a straight line with a pull action to assure more control to the return. Don't pull up. The weight should be completely forward.

5 Followthrough

Hold the followthrough just out in front, reaching toward the net. Then start your move back to the center of the court, using the proper footwork.

forehand return of serve

(footwork, deuce court)

1 Ready position

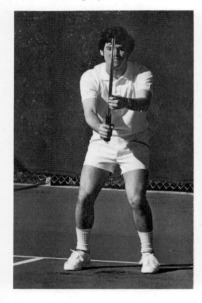

Assume the normal ready position for return of serve.

2 Step back

When you are crowded by a serve, bring your racket back, then move your non-stepping foot back quickly to get away from the ball.

3 Step in

Move in quickly with your stepping foot. Bring shoulders and hips around, shoulders stiff, wrist firm.

4 Step out

Racket back. As the ball moves away from you, step out with the right foot parallel to the baseline.

5 Step in

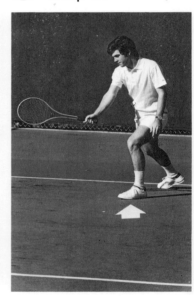

Move in quickly with your stepping foot to get weight forward. Wrist firm. Meet the ball early. Always try to cut the angle off the ball.

forehand return of serve
(footwork, ad court)

1 Ready position

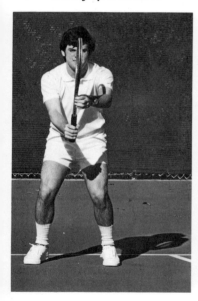

Assume the normal ready position for return of serve.

2 Step back

When you are crowded by a serve, **move your non-stepping foot back** quickly to get away from the ball.

3 Step in

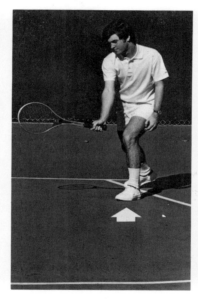

Move in quickly with your stepping foot. Bring shoulders and hips around, shoulders stiff, wrist firm.

4 Step out

Racket back. As the ball moves away from you, step out with the right foot parallel to the baseline.

5 Step in

Move in quickly with your stepping foot to get weight forward. Wrist firm. Meet the ball early. Always try to cut the angle off the ball.

backhand return of serve

(footwork, deuce court)

1 Ready position

Assume the normal ready position for return of serve.

2 Step back

When you are crowded by a serve, bring your racket back, then move your non-stepping foot back quickly to get away from the ball.

3 Step in

Move in quickly with your stepping foot. Bring shoulders and hips around. Shoulders still and wrist firm.

4 Step out

Racket back. As the ball moves away from you, step out with the left foot parallel to the baseline.

5 Step in

Step in quickly. This will thrust your weight forward in proper attitude to enable you to meet the ball early and, as a result, reduce the angle of the ball. The wrist should remain firm.

backhand return of serve

(footwork, ad court)

1 Ready position

Assume the normal ready position for return of serve.

2 Step back

When you are crowded by a serve, bring your racket head back, then move your non-stepping foot back quickly to get away from the ball.

3 Step in

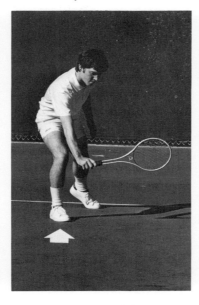

Move in quickly with your stepping foot. Bring shoulders and hips around. Shoulders still and wrist firm.

4 Step out

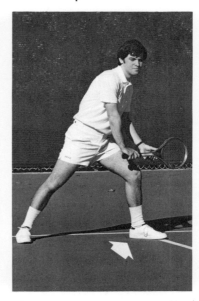

Racket back. As the ball moves away from you, step out with the left foot parallel to the baseline.

5 Step in

Step in quickly. This will thrust your weight forward in proper attitude to enable you to meet the ball early and, as a result, reduce the angle of the ball. The wrist should remain firm.

53

TENNIS COURT

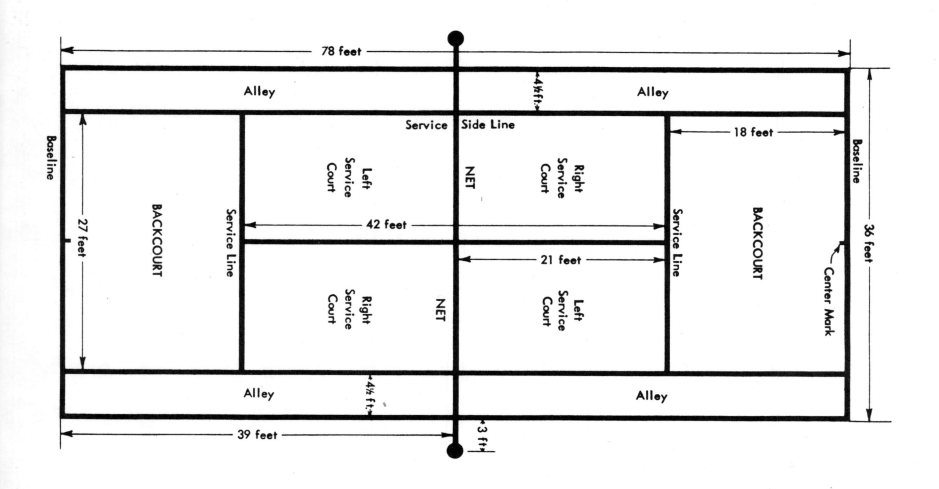

introduction to hitting
standard combinations

There are three basic combinations that properly executed will make up the largest part of your game. They are: (1) the cross court shot, (2) the down-the-line shot, and (3) the shot up the middle. Most natural of the three is the crosscourt stroke. Besides being hit over the lowest point of the net, it will also, when well hit, open up the court for a down-the-line follow-up.

The down-the-line shot, while somewhat more difficult, is used for exactly the opposite reason, it will leave your opponent vulnerable to the crosscourt placement.

The down-the-middle shot is usually used to keep the ball in play or to offer a change in strategy. It also reduces the passing angle from your opponent. .

The following pages discuss and illustrate the proper techniques to be used in hitting the various combinations.

forehand combinations

As discussed earlier, the forehand is your big gun. Most of your winners will come from this side. Remember: position your shoulders to point in the direction you plan to hit the ball and, once committed, don't change your mind in the middle of the stroke. Your body position will absolutely determine the direction of the ball.

1 The Crosscourt

Move into position to hit the ball with racket back, front shoulder pointing to the crosscourt side of your opponent. This will open up your body slightly and permit you to catch the ball sooner. Step, hit and follow through to crosscourt.

2 Down the middle

This hit comes off the basic ground stroke. Point your front shoulder in the direction of center court, a move that closes the body slightly. Make contact with the ball directly in front of your stepping foot and follow through directly in line with center court.

3 Down the line

Point the front shoulder down the line. Note how this positioning tends to close the body which in turn will enable you to stroke the down-the-line shot smoothly and accurately.

backhand combinations

The backhand is a more natural shot than the forehand but despite this, in your game plan, it will more often be used to set up the "winner" for the forehand. Practice the backhand combinations with this strategy in mind.

1 The Crosscourt

Move into position to hit the ball with racket back, front shoulder pointing to the crosscourt side of your opponent. This will open up your body slightly and permit you to catch the ball sooner. Step, hit and follow through to crosscourt.

2 Down the middle

This hit comes off the basic ground stroke. Point your front shoulder in the direction of center court, a move that closes the body slightly. Make contact with the ball directly in front of your stepping foot and follow through directly in line with center court.

3 Down the line

Point the front shoulder down the line. Note how this positioning tends to close the body which in turn will enable you to stroke the down-the-line shot smoothly and accurately.

serve combinations (deuce court)

When serving from the deuce court, position yourself close to the service center mark on the court. This will permit you to angle your serve wide or down the line. Obviously it is strategically sound to vary your serve so that your opponent will be unable to anticipate either the speed or direction of your serve. Remember, with the correct grip you will have a natural spin.

1 Hitting the wide serve

At the toss the shoulders should line up with the corner of the singles side line and the service line. This will permit the server to get around sooner and direct the ball more accurately. Should you wish to slice the serve, toss it more to the side.

2 Hitting down the middle

The strategy here is to crowd your opponent and thus to minimize the effectiveness of his return. To accomplish this, line your shoulders up at the toss to point directly at your opponent. With the correct toss, hit and follow through, the ball will spurt directly at your opponent.

3 Hitting down the line

Line up your shoulder with your opponent's center service line. This will close your body sufficiently to permit you to direct the ball at this center line. The turns as described here are made at the time of the toss and, as such, are not apparent to your opponent.

serve combinations (ad court)

For the ad court serve, position yourself about three feet from the service center mark. This will automatically set up the desirable angle to the wide side. For a righthander, this is the unnatural side because it forces you to hit across your body. To compensate for this, more serving practice should be concentrated on the ad court.

1 Hitting the wide serve

At the toss the shoulders should line up with the corner of the singles side line and the service line. This will permit the server to get around sooner and direct the ball more accurately. Should you wish to slice the serve, toss it more to the side.

2 Hitting down the middle

The strategy here is to crowd your opponent and thus to minimize the effectiveness of his return. To accomplish this, line your shoulders up at the toss to point directly at your opponent. With the correct toss, hit and follow through, the ball will spurt directly at your opponent.

3 Hitting down the line

Line up your shoulder with your opponent's center service line. This will close your body sufficiently to permit you to direct the ball at this center line. The turns as described here are made at the time of the toss and, as such, are not apparent to your opponent.

forehand volley combinations

The net volley is designed to cut off your opponent's shot and, hopefully, put the ball away. It is a stroke that enables you to take advantage of the most extreme angles, which, in turn, allows you to effectively "run" your opponent. Of course your shots must be accurate or in the net position you will be left vulnerable to the passing shot from your opponent.

1 Crosscourt volley

Face squarely in the direction of the on-coming ball. Catch the ball well out in front and close the racket head slightly to angle the ball to the crosscourt side.

2 Hitting down the middle

Stand facing directly down the middle of the court. Open the racket head and meet the ball out in front. Complete the volley stroke.

3 Hitting down the line

Line up your shoulders with the sideline thus closing the body. Now hit your normal volley stroke with the racket head open to guide the ball down the line.

backhand volley combinations

The backhand volley combinations serve exactly the same competitive function as do the forehand. They are designed to control your opponent's position and his game and, when the opportunity presents itself, you can make the winning shot. On the backhand volley, it is well to use the left hand as a racket stabilizer.

1 Crosscourt volley

Face squarely in the direction of the on-coming ball. Catch the ball well out in front and close the racket head slightly to angle the ball to the crosscourt side.

2 Hitting down the middle

Stand facing directly down the middle of the court. Open the racket head and meet the ball out in front. Complete the volley stroke.

3 Hitting down the line

Line up your shoulders with the sideline thus closing the body. Now hit your normal volley stroke with the racket head open to guide the ball down the line.

forehand combinations

(return of serve, deuce court)

The forehand return of serve may be a power stroke. It can be used to pass your opponent if he is moving to net, or to hit deep to keep him at the baseline if he elects to stay back.

1 The Crosscourt

As the ball approaches, open the shoulders and make contact out in front of the forward foot. As contact is made, the front shoulder should be pointed in the direction of your anticipated return. Hit straight through the ball, rotating shoulders, torso and hips, while pointing the racket head for the crosscourt shot.

2 Hitting down the middle

To play the ball down the middle, close the body slightly so that the front shoulder is pointing in the direction of the anticipated shot. Step and hit, making contact at the front toe. As contact is made, rotate shoulders, torso and hips to insure proper followthrough.

3 Hitting down the line

Close the shoulders so that the front shoulder is pointing down the line. Make contact ahead of the front toe. Rotate shoulders, torso and hips around and follow through down the line.

forehand combinations
(return of serve, ad court)

The forehand return of serve in the ad court is likewise a power stroke. Properly executed, it will take away much of the advantage of your opponent's serve.

1 The Crosscourt

2 Hitting down the middle

3 Hitting down the line

As the ball approaches, close the shoulders and make contact out in front of the forward foot. As contact is made, the front shoulder should be pointed in the direction of your anticipated return. Hit straight through the ball, rotating shoulders, torso and hips, while pointing the racket head for the crosscourt shot.

To play the ball down the middle, open the body slightly so that the front shoulder is pointing in the direction of the anticipated shot. Step and hit, making contact at the front toe. As contact is made, rotate shoulders, torso and hips to insure proper followthrough.

Open the shoulders so that the front shoulder is pointing down the line. Make contact ahead of the front toe. Rotate shoulders, torso and hips around and follow through down the line.

63

backhand combinations
(return of serve, deuce court)

The backhand return of serve is best used as a placement stroke. As mentioned in the general discussion of the backhand, you can convert it into a winning part of your game but it will take more practice than for the forehand. Give it this additional attention. It will reward you many times.

1 The Crosscourt

As the ball approaches, close the shoulders and make contact out in front of the forward foot. As contact is made, the front shoulder should be pointed in the direction of your anticipated return. Hit straight through the ball, rotating shoulders, torso and hips, while pointing the racket head for the crosscourt shot.

2 Hitting down the middle

To play the ball down the middle, open the body slightly so that the front shoulder is pointing in the direction of the anticipated shot. Step and hit, making contact at the front toe. As contact is made, rotate shoulders, torso and hips to insure proper followthrough.

3 Hitting down the line

Open the shoulders so that the front shoulder is pointing down the line. Make contact ahead of the front toe. Rotate shoulders, torso and hips around and follow through down the line.

backhand combinations

(return of serve, ad court)

As you practice (and as you play for that matter) it is well to use your left hand for additional leverage on your racket.

1 The Crosscourt

As the ball approaches, open the shoulders and make contact out in front of the forward foot. As contact is made, the front shoulder should be pointed in the direction of your anticipated return. Hit straight through the ball, rotating shoulders, torso and hips, while pointing the racket head for the crosscourt shot.

2 Hitting down the middle

To play the ball down the middle, close the body slightly so that the front shoulder is pointing in the direction of the anticipated shot. Step and hit, making contact at the front toe. As contact is made, rotate shoulders, torso and hips to insure proper followthrough.

3 Hitting down the line

Close the shoulders so that the front shoulder is pointing down the line. Make contact ahead of the front toe. Rotate shoulders, torso and hips around and follow through down the line.

overhead combinations

The overhead is an often neglected shot, and when not neglected, misused. Club players, and many professionals for that matter, look upon the high flying ball as an object to be smashed. Seldom do they use touch and place it as they would a volley—and yet that is the way it should be used. In essence, the overhead is a serve that has already been tossed. Place it with the same care and direction.

1 The Crosscourt

Move into position with the ball in front. Point your shoulders in line with your planned hit crosscourt. Hit and follow through. Return to volley position.

2 Hitting down the middle

Aim the front shoulder down the middle, hit and follow through. Return to volley position.

3 Hitting down the line

Close the body to point the shoulder down the line, hit and follow through. Return to volley position.

introduction to some advanced techniques

This section of the *Courtside Companion* illustrates and describes difficult shots that require a great deal of practice and finesse. Even many accomplished players find difficulty in executing many of these strokes.

I strongly suggest that a player not attempt these strokes until he has become proficient in the basic strokes outlined in the earlier pages. Even then, it is best to add one or two at a time.

forehand dropshot

The dropshot is an extremely delicate shot. It is usually unwise to attempt it against a hard-hit ball, While it may be executed from any spot on the court, it is often made more effectively from inside the service court.

1 The Backswing

As you take the racket back, turn shoulders, torso and hips to arrive at a position sideways to the net. Position the left hand over the left thigh but opposite the grip. Keep eyes on the ball and weight on the back foot.

2 Move to the ball

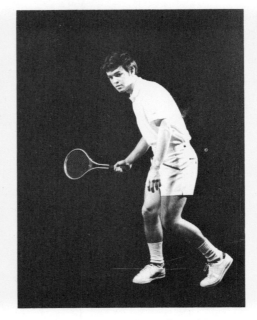

Move into a normal forehand (or backhand) position, dropping the racket head down to the level of the ball. Open the racket head slightly so that the lower portion of the racket frame will arrive at the ball first.

3 The Hit

Contact should be made well out in front of the forward foot. Racket head should be open, eyes on the ball. At this point shoulders, torso and hips should have completed their rotation to about a 45° angle with the net. At the point of contact, the ball should be made to "sit" in the strings as the racket moves forward. Hold the follow-through. Properly executed, the ball will drop gently over the net.

backhand dropshot

The dropshot is an extremely delicate shot. It is usually unwise to attempt it against a hard-hit ball. While it may be executed from any spot on the court, it is often made more effectively from inside the service court.

1 The Backswing

As you take the racket back, turn shoulders, torso and hips to arrive at a position sideways to the net. Position the left hand over the left thigh but opposite the grip. Keep eyes on the ball and weight on the back foot.

2 Move to the ball

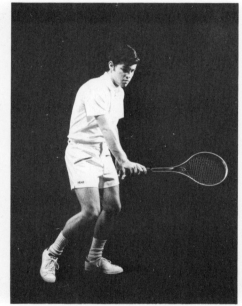

Move into a normal forehand (or backhand) position, dropping the racket head down to the level of the ball. Open the racket head slightly so that the lower portion of the racket frame will arrive at the ball first.

3 The Hit

Contact should be made well out in front of the forward foot. Racket head should be open, eyes on the ball. At this point shoulders, torso and hips should have completed their rotation to about a 45° angle with the net. At the point of contact, the ball should be made to "sit" in the strings as the racket moves forward. Hold the follow-through. Properly executed, the ball will drop gently over the net.

forehand drop volley

The drop volley is used as a change of pace or short placement from the volley position. Great touch is required to execute this shot. It should only be used when your opponent is out of position. Best results come off hard shots by your opponent.

1 Move to the ball

Position the racket head upward in proper volley position above the wrist. Keep the wrist loose, and the racket head well out in front of the body.

2 Contact

As the racket is brought into contact with the ball, allow the ball to settle into the strings by opening the racket head slightly. This will give backspin to the ball. The ball should drop just over the net.

backhand drop volley

As with the forehand, the backhand drop volley is used as a change of pace or short placement from the volley position. However, it is a more natural shot from the backhand due to the wrist being held less firmly, thus permitting better touch.

1 Move to the ball

Position the racket head upward in proper volley position above the wrist. Keep the wrist loose, and the racket head well out in front of the body.

2 Contact

As the racket is brought into contact with the ball, allow the ball to settle into the strings by opening the racket head slightly. This will give backspin to the ball. The ball should drop just over the net.

lob volley (forehand)

(backhand)

Strategy calls for the lob volley to be used when all players are at net. A well-executed lob will force your opponent to retreat and allow you to retain court position advantage. It is an advanced technique that requires great touch.

1 Move to the ball

Assume the normal volley position, shift weight forward, position racket head well out in front.

2 The Hit

Cup the wrist under, open the racket head to allow the ball to hit the strings and arc over your opponent. The wrist should be firm and the shoulders stiff. A good "punch" action is the proper contact motion for the lob volley.

1 Move to the ball

Assume the normal volley position, shift weight forward, position racket head well out in front.

2 The Hit

Cup the wrist under, open the racket head to allow the ball to hit the strings and arc over your opponent. The wrist should be firm and the shoulders stiff. A good "punch" action is the proper contact motion for the lob volley.

half volley (forehand)   (backhand)

The half volley is primarily a defensive shot that telegraphs to your opponent your inability to move to net in time to volley. It requires great skill and timing and must be executed low to the court.

1 Move to the ball

From the volley position, crouch low to the ball with knees bent. Keep wrist firm and thrust the racket head down to the ball. Your weight should be forward. Now block the ball with the racket head squared to the ball.

2 The Hit

Make contact with the ball out in front of the body. Roll the arm over and hit through the ball to keep it low.

1 Move to the ball

From the volley position, crouch low to the ball with knees bent. Keep wrist firm and thrust the racket head down to the ball. Your weight should be forward. Now block the ball with the racket head squared to the ball.

2 The Hit

Make contact with the ball out in front of the body. Roll the arm over and hit through the ball to keep it low.

forehand approach

1 Ready position

Assume the ready position. The approach shot is an offensive weapon to be used when you have forced your opponent to hit short. You have had to give up your baseline and rather than get caught in the middle of the court, hit this shot and move in to volley. It is best to hit deep or down the line.

2 The Backswing

Take a quick step out to the side. Turn the body slightly by pivoting on the balls of the feet and rotating the shoulders, torso and hips.

3 Move to the ball

Keep your racket out to the side of the body but not all the way back.

4 The Hit

The hit comes with the front foot leading. It consists of a "push-like" motion with contact being made at the peak of the bounce. Hit deep to the backcourt.

5 Followthrough

Follow through about head-high, pointing to your shot. Continue in to net and set for a volley.

backhand approach

1 Ready position

2 The Backswing

3 Move to the ball

4 The Hit

5 Followthrough

Assume the ready position. The approach shot is an offensive weapon to be used when you have forced your opponent to hit short. You have had to give up your baseline and rather than get caught in the middle of the court, hit this shot and move in to volley. It is best to hit deep or down the line.

Take a quick step out to the side. Turn the body slightly by pivoting on the balls of the feet and rotating the shoulders, torso and hips.

Keep your racket out to the side of the body but not all the way back.

The hit comes with the front foot leading. It consists of a ''pull-like'' motion with contact being made at the peak of the bounce. Hit deep to the backcourt.

Follow through about head-high, pointing to your shot. Continue in to net and set for a volley.

serve and volley

You achieve great advantage over an opponent with the capability to execute a good serve and volley. It is a potent offensive weapon.

Serve well, hit to the open court and cover your first volley. These are the ingredients. But it takes patience and practice to make them all work together.

In the following examples, the server will be hitting a wide serve and covering the wide side.

serve and volley (deuce court)

1 The Serve

Following the serve, continue a long reach forward with the racket, bring the back foot around and complete the stroke with a good stride into the court.

2 First set

Move to net in the area of the service line and set your feet about shoulder-width apart.

3 First volley

Make your first volley to open court to prevent your opponent from returning crosscourt or down the line.

4 Second set

This set should cover your first volley. If the first shot was properly executed in all probability you will be given a put away opportunity as your opponent returns the ball. Be positioned and prepared for it.

5 Second volley

This is the put away shot that you have set up by maneuvering your opponent out of position.

serve and volley (ad court)

1 The Serve

Following the serve, continue a long reach forward with the racket, bring the back foot around and complete the stroke with a good stride into the court.

2 First set

Move to net in the area of the service line and set your feet about shoulder-width apart.

3 First volley

Make your first volley to open court to prevent your opponent from returning crosscourt or down the line.

4 Second set

This set should cover your first volley. If the first shot was properly executed in all probability you will be given a put away opportunity as your opponent returns the ball. Be positioned and prepared for it.

5 Second volley

This is the put away shot that you have set up by maneuvering your opponent out of position.

the crowded volley

This shot is required to defend against the direct shot at the midsection when stationed at net. It is impossible to hit the normal forehand volley because the body would interfere with arm motion. As a result, the player must place the racket as a shield to protect his waist.

1 Moving and hitting

Place the racket head square to the ball and out in front of the body. Elbows out. The body will be facing the net and, if possible, have the weight forward.

2 Hit and followthrough

Hit to the open court with a forearm punch motion. Keep the wrist firm and drive the racket head out to the side on the followthrough.

backpedal overhead

The backpedal overhead is used mostly as a defensive shot because the need for it occurs only when a player is out of position.

To make the play, retreat rapidly, using the non-hitting hand to follow the path of the ball. Position racket head in overhead posi-tion. Plant the back foot at the contact point. Flex the back leg and push off in a backward leap. Drive shoulders, torso and hips around. Make the hit while both feet are in the air, then complete the stroke on the front foot.

how to practice

Backboard practice

Many times practice on a backboard can be of greater benefit than practicing with another player. But to make it pay dividends, you must concentrate on correct positioning and proper form.

Step 1. Stand sideways to the board with racket back knee-low.

Step 2. With the non-hitting hand, hold the ball out in front of the body in the direction of the board.

Step 3. Drop-hit the ball using proper form.

Step 4. Catch the ball as it comes back to you. Repeat five or 10 times to get the feel.

Step 5. Following the same procedure, hit the ball twice. Continue until you develop a rhythm.

Step 6. Continue to practice, building the number of "good form" returns. Do not continue hitting if you lose your rhythm. Stop and begin again.

Practice with another player

If a player equally dedicated as you is available, this is the best way to practice. It is best to have six to 12 balls to work with.

Player A begins the rally, using proper form. *Player B* returns the ball, using proper form. This sequence should be repeated five to 10 times.

Player A begins the rally again. *Player B* returns the shot. Player A returns the ball to B. Continue until you can rally ten times without missing and using the proper form.

The same practice program should be used with the backhand.

Competitive practice ideas

Play a Pro Set. Score in the traditional way, but play an 8-game set. Player must win by two games.

Play points. Play to 21 points instead of regular match. Change serve every five points. You must win by two or more points.

Tie-breaker practice. When a set is tied at 6-all, play the best of nine points. Players alternate serving two points. They change sides after the fourth point. One player serves the remaining three points, while the receiver is allowed his choice of ad or deuce court in which to receive the third point if it is required.

Even the sides. There is very little practice or enjoyment if competitors are unequal in skill. This can be evened out and the situation made more competitive by giving the less qualified player two options: either spot him one game and serve or begin each game at 15 love or 30 love.

drills (for fun and finesse)

The baseline, three-hit

This is a baseline drill which is initiated with a ground stroke. The ball must then be hit over the net three times before the point officially starts. Beginning with the fourth time the ball crosses the net, the person winning the point counts one. Continue at baseline until one player wins 11 points.

The short court drill

Players must keep within the service court area. Use touch and angle shots to win points. Play to either 21 or 31. May be done with volleys.

Deep shot drill

Play the same as with the baseline three-hit, except the ball cannot drop in the service court without loss of point. Play to either 21 or 31 points.

Crosscourt

Player puts the ball in play with a ground stroke. Players then attempt a continuous crosscourt rally. The three-hit rule is optional. Play to 21 or 31 points.

Down the line

Play is initiated with a ground stroke. Play must continue down the line. Score 21 or 31 points.

Half court

Initiate play with ground stroke. Players must keep the ball in play within the half court area, extending the center service line to the baseline.

Hit and volley

To develop elementary volley skill, have one player at the net and one player at baseline. Use three hit rule. Change position after every five strokes. Length of game optional.

Goof game

For four players, a baseline game: "A" hits to "B" who hits to "C" who hits to "D" in sequence. Each player begins play with 10 points and each time a player makes a "goof" he loses a point. The winner is the player with the most points when one of the other players has lost all of his.

Serve one

Play regular game and regular set, but allow one serve rather than two.

Controlled smash

A game to develop the lob and overhead. One player sends the lob and the other returns with a controlled overhead. They then reverse the procedure. Continue until one player has 21 points.

Crunch

For four players. One team is at net, the other at baseline. Baseline team begins play with a ground stroke to the volleyer who volleys the ball deep. The point is then in play as the baseline team tries to lob over the net team, the net team tries to knock off the lob. If lob is successful the net players must return the ball and get back to net. The baseline team may only lob. Score 11 or 21 points.

Pass drill

Players positioned as in the hit and volley drill. Use the three-hit drill. The player at baseline tries to pass the one at net. Use both half court and full court. Play to 11 or 21. No lobbing allowed.

Rapid volley

Hit or be hit. One player stands at service line and hits five or ten balls directly one after another. Later, move back to the baseline and repeat. Advance the game by having the volleyer run to net, stop, set and volley.

tips on winning

Books have been written on this subject and undoubtedly others are in preparation, therefore only a few key reminders have been included in the *Courtside Companion*.

1. If the opportunity presents itself, watch at least one set of your opponent's play before you meet him.

2. Play the percentages, especially if you are behind.

3. Concentrate. Concentrate. Concentrate.

4. Never consider for a moment that you won't be the winner.

5. Never change a winning game; always change a losing one.

6. Give everything you've got to the first few games. Win early and it will shake your opponent's confidence and bolster your own.

7. Keep your head. Too many players beat themselves.

8. Learn to play under all conditions—wind, cold, poor surfaces, sun.

9. Don't beg. When closing in on a set or match don't wait for your opponent to make a mistake; win the point for yourself. Beggars often become losers.

10. Don't press. Always play your own game.

11. If you do lose a match, review your mistakes in your mind so that you don't repeat them.

12. Make each loss as well as each win a stepping stone to success.

etiquette

Perhaps no other sport operates under such a demanding code of ethics and sportsmanship as does tennis. With its rapid growth and the ability of players to make large sums of money, this protective cloak is rapidly being torn away, but it is unlikely that it will ever sanction the cheers, boos, catcalls or movement by spectators during play that is in evidence in other sports. And in the opinion of the author, it should not.

With regard to spectators

Remain seated and quiet during play. Never call a match from the stands or vocally contest the call of either player or linesmen. Applaud a good shot, hold applause on errors. Move in and out of your seat or court area only during change of sides by players.

With regard to players

When your ball rolls to another court, retrieve only between points. Return stray balls that enter your court immediately. Don't rush play, be certain your opponent is ready. Make your calls distinct. If in doubt, play two. The server is always responsible for the score. Always be courteous. Congratulate your opponent if he wins.

Always dress in proper attire. Observe the court and relinquish when your time is up without being asked.

Tournament etiquette

Report to your match earlier than the scheduled time even though there is a default allowance. If you are the winner return the balls to the score table and turn in your scores. Be prepared to call lines if asked. Always thank the tournament committee and your hostess for their consideration.

scoring

Scoring is important to determine the winner of a game, set or match. Scoring is also important to the serious player for historical reasons. It will show him strengths and weaknesses and will also be a record of performance against players with whom he may again be paired.

For the uninitiated, a simple scoring system is as follows:

First point won by a player is called 15, the second point won is called 30, the third is called 40, and the next point won by a player gives him the game. The opposing player's score is called at love until he wins a point, at which time he is scored in the same manner as his opponent.

When the score is tied at "40 all," it is called *deuce*. A player then must win *two* consecutive points to win the game. The first point won after deuce is called *advantage*. If the player who has the advantage loses the next point, the score reverts to deuce and once more the player must win two consecutive points.

A *set* consists of at least six games. The player who has first won six games wins the set, provided his opponent has not won more than four games. If the opponent has won five games it is then deuce and the same procedure must be followed in determining a winner as in a deuce game unless a tie-breaker is in effect. In this event, the following scoring procedure should be used:

At *six all* continue the normal service rotation. Player A serves points 1 and 2. Player B serves points 3 and 4. They then change sides of the court without pause. Player A now serves points 5 and 6 followed by B who serves points 7, 8 and 9 if necessary.

In the event the 9th point is necessary, player A may select the court in which he would like to receive the serve.

To initiate play in the second set, the player who received the serve first in the tie-break begins the service.

If the sets are tied "one set all" the players shall spin the racket having agreed upon a marking on the racket to determine serve or side in the final set.

A *match* is generally two out of three sets except in important championship matches where play is usually three out of five sets.

quick check list

The Grip
1. Shake hands with the racket for the forehand grip.
2. Point "V" of the thumb and forefinger is on top of racket.
3. Palm of the hand faces the net on forehand grip.
4. Hold grip in the middle of the leather.
5. Index finger knuckle is up, looking at you, on the backhand grip.
6. Don't make a fist. Relax the grip and keep fingers somewhat spread.

The Stance
1. Face the net.
2. Bounce on your toes.
3. Hold racket level with your chin.
4. Flex knees, weight forward.

The Backswing
1. When you turn, racket goes back.
2. Turn shoulders, torso and hips to sideways position.
3. Racket comes back knee low.
4. Keep wrist and shoulder stiff.
5. Pivot the body and racket as one.
6. The arm should be straight and stiff.
7. Wrist set back. (Note wrinkles at wrist.)
8. Point shoulder at ball as it bounces.
9. Racket should be back before the ball bounces.

Step and hit forward motion
1. Step into ball, shift weight from the rear to the front foot.
2. Make contact even with the front toe.
3. On the followthrough, the racket should finish in the direction of the ball at about head-high.
4. At the finish, player should be square to the net.
5. Stroke the ball, don't slap at it.
6. Keep the wrist firm.
7. Bend the knees slightly through the hit, then come up to a straighter position on the followthrough.
8. Always be in position for your next shot.

Serve
1. Grip the racket half way between the forehand and backhand grips.
2. Hold the grip at the middle of the leather.
3. Righthanders point the left toe to the right net post, lefthanders the opposite.
4. Arms go down together, up together.
5. Drop racket low, behind the back, with hand close behind the ear.
6. Toss the ball over the toe of front foot.
7. Reach up and out for the ball.
8. Bring weight from the rear foot to the front foot at the toss.
9. Give tremendous wrist snap at contact with the ball.
10. Follow through.

some tennis terms

Ace: An earned point on the serve in which the opponent fails to contact the ball with his racket.

Advantage: A point scored after deuce.

Ad Court: Lefthand court.

Alley: Part of the court lying between side-lines.

Baseline: Back line at either end of the court.

Backhand: Stroking the ball on the left side of the body for a right-hand player, the opposite for a left-hand player.

Blading Racket: Angling the racket in a manner that, when brought in contact with the ball, it will produce underspin.

Crosscourt: A ball driven across the court from one corner to the extreme opposite corner.

Deuce Court: The side of the court from which play is initiated.

Double Fault: Two successive faults by server.

Doubles: Two players on each side of the court.

Dropshot: A ball hit with delicate touch that just drops over the net.

Fault: A served ball that fails to land in the proper court.

Forehand: Racket stroking the ball on the right side of the body for a right-hand player, opposite for a left-hand player.

Ground Stroke: Stroke used to strike the ball after it has bounced.

Half Serve: The serve is initiated with the racket behind the head.

Let: A ball or point that is to be replayed on serve.

Lob: A ball hit in the air over an opponent's head.

Love: A scoring term indicating nothing, or zero.

Net Ball: A ball that hits the net and still crosses into opponent's court.

Overspin: Stroke made with racket head closed to bring racket over the top of the ball.

Placement: Hitting the ball to a pre-determined point on the court.

Racket Face:

Flat: Racket face in vertical angle to the ground.

Open: Racket face is slanted back and away from vertical angle.

Closed: Racket face is slanted forward and toward the ground.

Rally: An exchange of shots.

Serve: Putting the ball into play by tossing it into the air and stroking it.

Service Court: The area into which a ball is served.

Set: A series of games.

Smash: A fast overhead stroke intended to kill the ball by speed and placement.

Tie Breaker: Scoring used when games in a set are tied at six all.

Underspin: A stroke made with racket head open to cut under the ball.

Volley: A stroke made by hitting the ball before it has touched the playing court.

index

acknowledgments

In appreciation for their professional guidance
and personal friendship,
my thanks to —

J. Paul Wilkins, Executive Professional
Sun Valley, Idaho

Butch Krikorian, Tennis Coach
San Jose State

and to

Gerald L. French • Photography
Patterson & Hall • Cover design
Head Ski Company • Tennis racket and apparel
Craig Isaacs • Model